Sandhurst Occasio

No 2

# Military Justice in the Georgian Army: the Trial of Colonel James Butler, 1828

## Dr Peter Thwaites

Royal Military Academy Sandhurst

2010

## THE TRIAL OF COLONEL JAMES BUTLER, 1828

Staring down from above the door leading out of the Grand Entrance into the west corridor of Old College is the portrait of a stern faced grey haired man in an Ordnance Corps uniform. In January 2001 the Academy purchased this portrait in oils said, by the previous owners, to be of Colonel James Butler by Sir George Hayter (1792-1871), painted in about 1800. Clearly either the attribution to the artist or the date was incorrect, because in 1800 Hayter would have been 8 years old! In fact the quality of the painting suggests a lesser artist than Hayter, who was appointed Queen Victoria's portrait and history painter in 1837. There was also no evidence, apart from family tradition, that the sitter was indeed Colonel James Butler, though the uniform seemed to be of the right period. But, as Curator of the Sandhurst Collection, I still recommended that the Academy bought the portrait, because of the importance of the reputed sitter to the early history of Sandhurst.

Indeed, when the Junior Department of the Royal Military College (RMC), one of the direct ancestors of the current RMAS, was established in 1802, Butler was amongst its first members of staff. He was probably born in March 1759 and came from an Anglo Irish family who lived in Priestown House, near Dunboyne, County Meath, which had been in the family since the time of Edward II. As was traditional for families at that period, the eldest son inherited the house and lands, the next son joined the Church and later became Rector of Burnchurch, County Kilkenny, while the younger son, James, was destined for a career in the army. He joined the Royal Military Academy, Woolwich as a Gentleman Cadet on 1 October 1772 and was commissioned into the Royal Artillery on 11 January 1776. The following year he was posted to North America where he served for two years. In 1793 Butler joined the newly formed Royal Horse Artillery and in 1794 was commanding F Troop RHA. He seems to have spent the next few years in England and did not see active service in the war against Revolutionary France[1].

Colonel Butler joined the Royal Military College at Great Marlow on 4 March 1802 as Superintendent at a salary of £290 per annum. He was to act as Commandant "to direct studies, and to be responsible for discipline and interior government"[2], while the founder of the College, Colonel John Gaspard Le Marchant , as Lieutenant Governor, handled the administrative affairs of both the Senior and Junior Departments of the RMC. In August 1811, already confirmed as Commandant, Butler replaced Le Marchant, as Lieutenant Governor of the Junior Department, on the latter's promotion to Major General, and the posts of Commandant and Lieutenant Governor were combined.

As Superintendent and later Commandant, Butler was responsible for the discipline of the Gentlemen Cadets. This was no easy task. The status of the Gentlemen Cadets was ambiguous. They were attending an establishment run by soldiers and were supposedly training for a career as army officers. But on the other hand they were paying fees for their tuition and had not taken the King's shilling. They could, therefore, be withdrawn by their family at any time. Indeed, many of them were taken out of the College well before they had completed their studies, either to take up a commission in the army purchased for them by their families, or to join another profession with the benefit of the academic education provided at the RMC. This made it difficult to impose discipline on a group of young men, aged 13 to 18, who knew they could leave the College at any time without damaging their future career prospects.

The first major disciplinary problem erupted in the summer of 1804, when a group of nine cadets mutinied, apparently in response to the actions of an over zealous Company Officer. The mutiny failed and the cadets were expelled[3]. Butler was commended by General Lord Harcourt, the Governor of the College at the time, for the prompt way he and his colleagues dealt with the attempted mutiny. Unfortunately an outbreak of disrespectful graffiti in 1806 caused the college authorities to remind the cadets of what had happened to those mutineers. The cadets responded by adding the words Rebellion and Mutiny to the graffiti, and both threats and violence were offered to members of the civilian academic staff. Le Marchant heard of this indiscipline and raised it at the next meeting of the Collegiate Board, laying the blame firmly on Colonel Butler. Butler was, however, vigorously defended by Harcourt. Alan Shepperd, in his history of Sandhurst, claims that Butler was an ally of General Harcourt's, and helped him to block some of Le Marchant's plans for the College[4]; so it may have been in Harcourt's interest to defend Butler. Yet another attempted mutiny in 1810, which included the production of a scurrilous pamphlet, which the author had the nerve to send to Butler, and a refusal of some cadets in B Company to parade, shows that discipline was indeed poor at Great Marlow[5]. Later, once the Junior Department had moved into its new buildings at Sandhurst, a number of clashes with the locals took place. A riot broke out at Eversley in 1819 and the annual Blackwater Fair usually led to fights between the cadets and the local youths[6], despite the best efforts of the College staff.

Michael Yardley, in his book on Sandhurst, firmly puts the blame for these breakdowns in discipline onto the shoulders of James Butler. He goes on to claim that Butler "had abused his position to line his own pockets and further the careers of incompetent, but well connected cadets to whose families he ingratiated himself" [7]. It is certainly true that Butler knew how to ingratiate himself to the rich and powerful. A copy of a letter has survived in the Butler family's archive from Dorothea Bland (1762-1816). Popularly known as Mrs Jordan, she was a famous Irish actress and from 1791 until 1811 the mistress of the Duke of Clarence (1765-1837), the future King

William IV. In the letter, Mrs Jordan presents her best compliments to Colonel and Mrs Butler and says she is "desired by HRH the Duke of Clarence to request their acceptance of the accompanying Urn of Plate (decorated on one side with the Royal arms and on the other with the arms of the Butlers of Dunboyne) together with his acknowledgements for their attentions to himself and kindness to dear George." [8] 'Dear George' was George Augustus Frederick Fitz-Clarence (1794-1842), later Earl of Munster, who was the eldest of three sons of the Duke of Clarence and Mrs Jordan, who were to be Gentlemen Cadets at the Royal Military College while Butler was there.

The charge that Butler furthered the careers of incompetent but well connected cadets is based on an incredible incident that marred the latter years of Butler's time at Sandhurst. It grew out of an attempt to save some money. In February 1828 John Cassaigne, a clerk in the Lieutenant Governor's office, resigned to take up a post in a London insurance company. Butler suggested to the then Governor of the College, General Sir Edward Paget, that they should replace him with a bandsman called Philip Clark who was reaching retirement age. Paget decided, however, to save money by moving Cassaigne's brother, Charles, who was Paget's own clerk and who had previously spent eight years as Butler's clerk, back into the Lieutenant Governor's office where he could work for Butler while continuing to draw up the Governor's official letters. But, when informed of the proposed change, Charles Cassaigne told Paget that Butler "was guilty of such malpractices of such peculations and frauds that no consideration on earth would induce him to remain at the College, if he was forced to go back into the Lieutenant Governor's office" [9]. Paget felt he had no option but to insist that Cassaigne detailed his charges against Butler, which Cassaigne did within the week in a letter dated 4 March 1828. The long document he produced was then sent by Paget to General Lord Hill, Commander of the Army, for his consideration on 16 March 1828.

The charges were discussed at the next meeting of the Supreme Board of the Royal Military College on 29 March, chaired by Lord Palmerston, who was then Secretary of State for War, and the Board decided that the charges were so serious that they should be considered in detail[10]. There followed a series of three meetings of the Board over the next few months at which evidence was taken from those involved and Butler was given an opportunity to answer the charges[11].

The charges made by Cassaigne concerned a number of issues, but covered four main areas[12]. The first was that Butler blatantly favoured some cadets at the expense of others, and suborned other members of staff to aid him in this. The second, related charge was that Butler, contrary to College regulations, accepted gifts from the families of those cadets that he favoured. Thirdly he was accused of making use of College resources, both human and material for his own private purposes, and lastly he was also accused of granting contacts to some local suppliers, even though they were not offering the cheapest or best service to the College, with the clear implication that Butler was receiving some kind of remuneration in return.

Two of the accusations did not stand up to close scrutiny and were quickly put aside. It was clear that Butler did receive occasional gifts of game and bottles of wine or whisky from grateful parents, though Butler, in his defence, claimed that it usually cost him more in paying for the postage, when the packages arrived, than the gifts were worth[13]. There was, though, the notable example quoted above of the gift from the Duke of Clarence. But, the Board could hardly criticise a brother of the King, and argued that that particular present was "much to the honour of the Lieutenant Governor" [14]. By inference, then, such gifts as the occasional pheasant or bottle of wine seemed of little importance, and merely reflected well on him. The Board refused to take this charge seriously, based on the evidence it had seen so far, and challenged Cassaigne to produce further concrete examples. This he could not do.


It was also clear that the charge of favouring some suppliers over others to the detriment of the College was impossible to prove. Cassaigne had specifically accused Butler of forcing the College canteen to buy supplies from someone recommended by Butler, and also of stopping the Clerk of Works from checking the quality of building supplies purchased for the College; the inference here being that Butler was letting contracts with suppliers who might be supplying shoddy building materials. However, the letting of supply contracts was the responsibility of the Collegiate Board on which the Governor as well as Butler sat. Cassaigne could not show, therefore, that Butler alone could give a supplier a contract, and when challenged on this point by the Board withdrew the accusation and claimed that he never intended to imply that Butler was gaining anything by changing contractor, just that he was not looking out for the best interests of the College. Butler, in his defence, also agreed that these were all Collegiate Board decisions, but said that he was happy to admit that he supported the letting of contracts to contractors who might not be the cheapest, but gave good quality food and other supplies, otherwise, he argued, they would be adopting a system more suitable for "a Jail or a Workhouse"[15]. Butler also claimed that the changes of practice concerning the Clerk of Works were intended to ensure that an independent check, by the Quarter Master, was kept on such materials, otherwise the Clerk of Works would be responsible for ordering, checking and using the materials[16]. The Board accepted his explanation, and could not find anything here worth examining further.


The other two charges were much more serious and occupied the majority of the Board's time. The first charge, of favouring some cadets over others and of furthering the careers of incompetent cadets seemed the most damning, particularly as Cassaigne could apparently produce proof. He laid before the Board copies of two letters Butler had written on 13 December 1821 to the families of two former cadets. In the first letter Butler claimed that he had used his influence to get their son passed by the Board of Examiners, and in the second that he had withheld information concerning the other cadet's poor disciplinary record from the Board. To gain a commission with a College recommendation required that the Gentlemen Cadets successfully completed the RMC course and passed an oral examination held in what is now Topper's Bar above the Grand Entrance of Old College. The teaching and assessing of the cadets were in the hands of the academic and military staff, and the final examination was before members of an Examining Board. But, despite Butler apparently being convicted by his own words, and failing to explain them when called on to defend his actions[17], the Board quickly dismissed this charge as well because Butler was not one of the examiners and the examining body was not supposed to take any account of recommendations from the staff of the College, but to judge the cadets on their performance in the examination. There could be no way, therefore, at least in theory, that Butler could have used his influence on a particular cadet's behalf. So either this was just an example of Butler toadying up to the families of the richer cadets and claiming credit where no credit was due, or the examination system was not as open and honest as it was claimed to be. Not surprisingly, the Board seems to have chosen to accept the former explanation for Butler's letters.

There was however a minor part of this charge which seemed to have more basis in fact. Cassaigne claimed that Butler had favoured some cadets in the monthly mathematics examinations. To progress through the College the cadets had to pass a series of examinations in different subjects. Of these, Cassaigne claimed, the mathematics examinations were the most important, because, he said, "upon his progress in (mathematics) much of the character of a cadet for ability, and of his means of ultimately getting a commission depend" [18]. The system was that the subject masters would set the examination and then once the results were in, the senior subject master would take a list of names to the Lieutenant Governor with recommendations marked in pencil as to who should be promoted into the next class and who should not. After consultation with Butler, the recommendations would be inked in and the pass list prepared.

Cassaigne claimed that on several occasions Thomas Laybourn, the Professor of Mathematics, was heard to exclaim that Butler had insisted that Laybourn passed cadets who were not up to standard while refusing to pass other cadets who were. Cassaigne claimed that Laybourn put up with this scandalous state of affairs because, for several years, he had rented out rooms in his house to those cadets who were unable to go home during vacations and that Butler had not only recommended his lodgings to the families of cadets, but had also authorised the use by Laybourn of College beds and linen for this purpose. The practice had only stopped when Laybourn had married a woman considered by the College authorities to be unsuitable and so cadets were no longer allowed to lodge with him[19]. The Board proceeded to take evidence from Laybourn who, perhaps unsurprisingly, denied everything. He stated that he had never complained about the Lieutenant Governor's decisions concerning who should pass and who should not. There were, Laybourn stated, a number of cases where cadets were borderline, having answered some questions well and others badly, and that in those circumstances he pencilled in his recommendation and sought the Lieutenant Governor's adjudication. Laybourn did admit that Butler had authorised his use of College beds and linen for his borders but claimed that it had only been the beds of those cadet who were staying with him, and that the beds and linen were returned to the College as soon as the vacations were over.

Another Master of Arithmetic, John Lowery, was called and he also claimed that Butler's interventions in the examination process were few and based on Butler's knowledge of the disciplinary record of the particular cadets, or on their length of stay. Lowery claimed that Butler had only ever once refused to pass a cadet whom Lowery thought worthy of promotion to the next class, and that was because of that particular cadet's terrible disciplinary record. Under cross examination from Butler, Lowery also conceded that Butler only recommended for promotion either cadets who had been passed over several times before, or orphans whose families could not afford to keep them at the College indefinitely. This charge also seemed, in the face of Laybourn's refusal to admit to his reported complaints about Butler, to be weak, though Cassaigne had found a former clerk in Butler's office, William Neyland, who told the Board that he had heard Laybourn making these complaints. But as Neyland had, according to the RMC Staff Register "absconded (from the RMC) in consequences of having involved himself in difficulties under disreputable circumstances" [20] in September 1823, his evidence probably carried little weight. The Board observed that the mathematics examinations did not, in fact, form the basis on which a recommendation for a commission was made, and so the matter was dropped, though the Board did order the minor amendment to College practice that in future the professors should ink in their original recommendation before submitting them for revision by the Lieutenant Governor.

Cassaigne had also claimed that Butler dealt more leniently with some cadets than with others, and fudged the punishment book to cover this up. Apparently cadets had been heard to claim that such and such a cadet could get away with indiscipline, while they would be punished for the same offence, and that the favoured cadets turned out to be those from aristocratic backgrounds. Here Cassaigne had the support of a junior Classics Master, Augustus Beevor, who was responsible for reporting on any indiscipline in the Halls of Study.

Beevor claimed that he had reported the indiscipline of a cadet named Beauclerk, the brother of a Lord, to Butler on several occasions, but that Butler had taken no action. Indeed the apparent leniency with which Beauclerk was treated had become such a scandal that cadets had complained to Beevor on a number of occasions about how unfair this was. But this accusation also failed, because the Governor, Sir Edward Paget, claimed in his statement to the Board that Butler had recommended the punishment of that particular cadet on a number of occasions, but the problem was that Beauclerk just did not respond to his correction. The Board did find noticeable discrepancies in the punishment book, and thought that it did seem that the same crime did not always merit the same punishment, but it merely made recommendations about how the book was to be maintained, and did not find that the discrepancies in the book or the punishments given out either showed that Butler was particularly at fault, or, indeed, proved the accusation of favouritism.

The Board then turned to Cassaigne's claims about misuse of College resources. He had made some minor claims about Butler having soda water bought for him by the College and having his private postage paid for from College funds. The first charge was easily answered by the College Surgeon, Ninian Bruce, who claimed that he considered Butler's health to be "precarious" because of his age, temperament and constitution, and that his medical condition required him to drink soda water. The clerk dealing with the College post could not say whether or not Butler did receive private parcels for which the College paid the postage because all post addressed to the Lieutenant Governor was delivered to Butler in the first instance and so it was impossible for any one else to tell which was official and which was private. Butler had already claimed that he paid the postage on parcels sent to him in his private capacity, and so the matter was dropped.

The more important charges, however, were more difficult to brush aside. Cassaigne claimed that Butler had used a College servant as his body servant and had rewarded the man by giving his wife a job as a nurse in the College detached hospital and by allowing them to live on the premises rent free. Butler was also accused of having used College servants to tend his garden, to look after his pigs, sheep and chickens and to cut wood for him from the College plantation. The subsequent examination of College servants by the Board revealed a cosy little arrangement by which Butler, the Adjutant and one or two other members of staff used College servants, supposedly during their own time or slack periods, to tend the gardens and allotments these members of staff had been allocated in the College grounds. A succession of servants admitted to the Board to working for Butler and others, usually for cash in hand or a share of the garden produce, on their gardens and allotments. But all claimed that, whether they have been ordered to do this by the College Quartermaster Sergeant, or had volunteered, the work was done after their College duties were completed or during the slack periods in vacations. Butler in his defence claimed that he needed to maintain several servants because of his position at the College and that he did so at his own expense. Occasionally the absence of one of his paid servants, or the demands of his garden meant that he did have to make use of College servants as volunteers during their own time, but that this was never to the detriment of their College duties, nor did he grant them special favours in return[21]. Given this unanimous claim that the work was outside of the servants' normal hours and did not interfere with their College work, the Board was unable to find fault with the arrangement.

There was, however, the question of the misappropriation of wood. The Clerk of Works, John Holman, told the Board that Butler had taken forty of fifty wooden boards, and the equivalent number of nails, over an eight year period to build a lean-to shed and a chicken house. Unfortunately for Cassaigne's attack on Butler, Holman admitted that the Governor had also used College wood to build a cow shed in his garden, and in fact the practice seemed rather too widespread throughout the College to single out Butler. But the Board did note that Butler was receiving wood cut from the estate for his own use. Butler, the Quartermaster Sergeant, the gardener, James Lambert and the various servants that had cut the wood, all claimed that Butler was only given the wood that was of such poor quality that it could not be sold. And Butler argued that the Governor knew he was receiving it, to which Paget agreed, claiming that he thought it was a long standing custom. But clearly the Board decided that it must draw the line somewhere. Butler was admonished for taking College assets for his private purposes and was ordered to pay for the wood he had used. And there the matter ended. Despite the many and various charges Cassaigne had laid against Butler, the lack of corroboration from the witnesses had meant that the Board was unable to find Butler at fault in any of the major matters and had only found him guilty of this very minor offence. Cassaigne left the College eighteen months later[22].

Butler had received very strong support during his trial from all the former Governors under whom he had served. Paget, indeed, claimed that "His Majesty does not possess an officer in his service who performs his duties with more anxious zeal, with more unremitting attention, or who has at heart more sincerely the public good" [23] than Butler. And Cassaigne had been unable, despite his mixture of evidence and innuendo, successfully to portrait Butler as a bloated spider at the centre of a web of corruption. Butler had emerged instead as a man who did a good job of running the College, but who also took advantage of the many perks that the job offered him, and was not averse to toadying up to some of the richer and more influential families of cadets. As such he was probably no worse than many other men of that time in similar positions, possibly including some of those sitting in judgement on him.

The trial does, however, provide an interesting insight into life at the Royal Military College during the decade after the end of the Napoleonic War. Clearly without any urgent pressure on the College to produce officers for the army, it was left to Butler and his military and academic staff to decide on how quickly a particular Gentleman Cadet could progress through the College towards his commission[24]. At that time the vast majority of those entering the Army purchased their commissions and families unhappy with the progress of their son through the College could always take that option, though it would seem that for some parents, at least, the College was providing their son with a good education and firm discipline, which was more valuable than a speedy transition to a future career. The College seems in this way to resemble the image of a modern American military school rather than the current Royal Military Academy Sandhurst which is its direct descendant.

Butler's trial also shows just how different in other ways the College was from the modern Academy. Although a military establishment, run by serving officers, Butler's trial shows that the College functioned more like a country estate. With the Governor's connivance, the officers on the College staff made use of College servants to help them with their quite extensive gardens and allotments, and drew on the estate's natural resources to make their lives more comfortable. Butler seems to have also gained some free medical treatment; though Cassaigne's attempt to portray him as taking more liberties with College resources than the others did not succeed, except, in the Board of Enquiry's opinion, for the claim that he misappropriated College wood.

While this trial paints perhaps a cosy picture of the RMC at that time, the next problem to strike Butler certainly did not. Just when Butler probably thought that his troubles were behind him, and that he could return to his duties and to his comparatively quiet life, a

The Trial of James Butler

series of disturbances broke out within the College over the period 15 to 24 October 1828. In the first incident some boys brought a local prostitute into the grounds and encouraged her to insult several of the Professors and Masters. One of the Mathematics Masters, Thomas Galloway, was so hurt by the insults that he considered resigning from the College, though he was later persuaded to stay[25]. In the second incident cadets shouted abuse at Masters living in the Terrace on the night of the King's birthday and stones were thrown at their houses on the night of the Blackwater Fair. During the same period Gentlemen Cadets gathered in the corridors by the Halls of Study before the evening study periods began kicking the Hall of Study doors, throwing stones and bottles into the Halls and letting off fireworks, as well as shouting and jeering and being insubordinate to Masters during the lessons. Masters were also abused in the grounds and in the Grand Entrance, and some cadets attempted to set fire to the heath land and plantations in front of Old College, and succeeded in burning down the Governor's Summer House.

Several boys were expelled and peace was restored. But the disturbances were serious enough to result in the calling of another board of enquiry. One of the members of the academic staff, John Turnpenny, a popular Master of History, Geography and Classics at the College, who had joined the staff in March 1816 after a brief military career in which he had distinguished himself, as a Lieutenant, by leading an attack by his regiment, the 48th Foot, at the Battle of Albuera, claimed that the disturbances were in part the result of collusion between the military staff and the cadets against the academic staff, because of unpopular changes that had been made by the Governor to the system of discipline at the College.

This system of discipline had originally been administered by the College's military staff. Minor offences were dealt with by the imposition of extra guard duties or drill, or confinement to the

College grounds. Insubordination could be punished by confinement in the isolation hospital and for disorderly behaviour boys could be sent to the Black Hole, an airless cell in the basement of Old College situated under the Grand Entrance, where they were kept for a few hours or a few days, depending on the severity of their crime, on bread and water. General Paget, however, now decided to revise the system of punishment, possibly to make it resemble that of a school rather than that of a military camp. Amongst the changes he introduced, the punishment for insubordination and disorderly behaviour was no longer to be solitary confinement in either the hospital or the Black Hole, but instead miscreants were to be given 'impositions' by the Masters to be completed within the evening. At first these impositions were unpopular amongst the boys, and some told the Chaplain, the Reverend William Wheeler, that they did not like being "removed out of the Officers' hands into the Masters" [26]. For their part, the Masters, led by Turnpenny, believed that the military staff was encouraging the boys to take out their displeasure on the Masters and Professors, because the officers resented losing control of the punishment of the boys. Turnpenny informed the Board of Enquiry that he could provide witnesses to prove this collusion. The College's Senior Major, Major Charles Wright, denied any collusion between his staff and the boys, though he admitted that relations between the military and academic staffs were soured by jealousy and had been bad "from time immemorial" [27].

In fact, although Turnpenny produced many witnesses for the Board, his case was not as easily proved as he had hoped. Some of the Masters gave examples of apparent collusion. Sergeants on duty in the corridors, for example, had on occasion, apparently, ignored outbreaks of violence against the Halls of Study doors, either literally turning their backs on the disturbances, or claiming that it was too dark for them to see who was responsible. At other times they pursued the culprits in such a tardy manner that the boys easily escaped. Then again, Masters claimed that, outside of study hours, the Sergeants seemed to be suspiciously absent from their posts whenever Masters were threatened or abused by cadets. Masters also accused the military officers of complicity in this campaign of abuse. Thomas Costin, a Military Drawing Master, claimed that the authority of the Professors and Masters was not supported by the Military Officers and he had been insulted by a boy in the presence of an officer, who had said nothing to the miscreant. On another occasion a Captain had walked out of the Grand Entrance on the approach of Turnpenny and another academic, later claiming that he thought they were about to be abused by some boys and did not want to appear complicit in this abuse. Another Captain, while removing a boy from a lesson for misconduct, at the request of a Master, was said to the boy, loudly enough for the whole class to hear, that he did not believe him to be guilty of any offence. But more importantly, the new system of discipline required the Captain on duty to hold any boy expelled from a lesson for misconduct at least until the end of that lesson. But Masters claimed that on many occasions boys were set free long before the lesson was over, and were then able to come and abuse the particular Master as he left the Hall of Study. Butler in reply said that the authority of the Masters was supported by the military and that while on occasions boys had been let out before the end of their impositions, this was only so that they should not miss the start of the next lesson.

Unfortunately for Turnpenny many of his witnesses refused to support his accusations against their military colleagues when in front of the Board, even though some at least seem to have provided him with relevant examples before the hearing took place. Indeed William De La Motte, the Drawing Master, who, Turnpenny claimed, had reported being insulted by cadets in the Grand Entrance in the presence of a Sergeant, stated that he had never had any problems with either the discipline of the boys or the cooperation of the military staff, though he did concede that the recent disturbances showed that discipline was now not as good as it had been ten years before. There was, indeed, a consensus amongst both the Masters and the military staff that discipline had deteriorated to some extent. The Reverend William Wheeler said that when he had arrived in 1804 discipline in the College was superior to that in public schools, but that now discipline had slackened. He blamed it on the indulgences granted to the boys, including allowing them to have tea in their dormitories, which had provided an opportunity for wine and spirits to be drunk by the boys out of sight of the staff. He also argued that cadets were having too much connection with loose women, whom, he argued, should be removed from the area by the local magistrates. He and other members of staff also claimed that an increasing number of boys were being sent to the College who had had poor disciplinary records at their previous schools. Butler in evidence before the Board claimed that on a number of occasions schools gave boys good reports, when in fact these boys had been in-disciplined while at the school. Clearly parents were sending badly behaved boys, with the connivance of their previous schools, to the RMC hoping that military discipline would succeed where ordinary discipline had failed.

In evidence, some of the masters, including Thomas Costin, who had been called a damned blackguard and bloody rascal by some cadets boating on the lake, claimed that they had reported abuses and disturbances to Butler and had had no reply. Thomas Galloway, one of the Mathematics masters, conceded that Butler had acted on his complaints, though had not seen fit to reply directly to him. Butler does not seem to have had a close relationship with his academic colleagues, and argued before the Board that the disciplining of the boys was not the Masters' concern and so there was no reason why he should inform them of what he had done in that regard. Butler may not have felt the Masters' complaints were particularly serious; though he claimed before the Board that he had done all he could to deal with these matters of insubordination and abuse. He clearly thought that the attacks on the estate were serious enough to warrant action, but he apparently felt that expelling the ringleaders was all that was needed. It is clear from his evidence to the Board that Butler carried out a rather half hearted review in the wake of these disturbances, in which he seems to have failed to question anyone. He was forced to admit to the Board of Enquiry that he had no idea of the cause of the disturbances, though he said he doubted that the new system of discipline was at their root because it had been introduced a full ten weeks before the disturbances had started. He felt a lot of the blame rested with the Junior Under Officers who failed to impose discipline amongst their fellow cadets, though he did also concede that he did not feel that the introduction of impositions in place of the use of the Black Hole had been beneficial to discipline. All in all his view was that disciplinary problems like this would arise now and then, particularly now that boys were arriving at the College at an older age.

In the face of the contradictory evidence presented by Turnpenny and his fellow academics, the Board of Enquiry found little to support the idea of a conspiracy between the military staff and the cadets, nor could it find any underlying cause for these disturbances. It also stated at the end of its deliberations that nothing on this occasion could warrant an observation to the prejudice of Colonel Butler "except that he does not seem to have exerted all the vigilance and energy, which circumstances called for from his situation" [28]. Clearly, however, all was not well within the College. The mutual jealousy between the academic and military staff, alluded to by both sides, coupled with an influx of some less than ideal cadets, sent to the College simply because other institutions had failed to control them, had caused discipline to collapse, and Butler's rather lethargic response had failed to get the situation under control. He retired shortly after this enquiry. Perhaps these two very public trials of his abilities and character within a few months had proved too much for him.

It may also have been that at 70 years of age Butler felt that his health would not stand up to any more strain. As the College doctor had claimed in evidence, Butler seems to have suffered with ill health through much of his tenure as Lieutenant Governor. Moreover, like so many unfortunate families of the period, Colonel Butler and his wife suffered the loss of several children, which must have taken a toll on him. His beloved children James, Catherine and Elizabeth died in their twenties at the College between 1817 and 1825 from illnesses "bravely borne" as he put on their memorials. They are buried in the Academy cemetery and remembered in memorials in the north lobby of the Royal Memorial Chapel; a grim reminder, perhaps, that the Royal Military College was not a healthy place to live at that time.

On the other hand, despite his trial and the two mild rebukes he had endured, Butler's military career did not suffer. He had officially retired from the Army on full pay in March 1819, having been promoted to Major General in June 1813, but remained the Lieutenant Governor at the RMC and indeed was promoted to Lieutenant General in May 1825. When he retired from the RMC on 24 March 1829, he was given command of the Royal Artillery Invalid Battalion. This unit held former gunners who were no longer capable of full military service, but were employed looking after the armaments and stores in fixed defences. He continued to appear in the Army List as their commander until his death on 18 August 1836 aged 77 (though his memorial says 74). Butler died at Holt Lodge, Kintbury in Berkshire (which survives today as a bed and breakfast hotel), which was possibly owned by another branch of the Butler family, as there were certainly land owners called Butler in the area at that time, though the Holt Lodge records from that period were destroyed long ago[29]. He is remembered in a memorial tablet "erected as a testimony of regard by his widow" [30], which is now located in a small alcove under the tower of the church of St Lawrence in nearby West Woodhay. The current church was built in 1883 on the site of the one that Butler would have known which burnt down, taking with it all the church's records, and the graves from the earlier church seem to have disappeared during the rebuilding of the new church. So, sadly, there is no known grave for this controversial figure that, for better or worse, played such a major part in the early history of Sandhurst.

## Notes

1. Askwith, W H, List of Officers of the Royal Regiment of Artillery 1716-1899, 4<sup>th</sup> Edition (!899), page 14. Duncan, F, History of the Royal Artillery Volume 1, John Murray (1872) page 400.

2. Anonymous, *Early records of the Royal Military College*, copy of an unpublished manuscript in the archive of the Sandhurst Collection, page 4.

3. Heathcote, T A and Evans, B D, The Story of Sandhurst, June 1978 page11

4. Shepperd, A, Sandhurst: The Royal Military Academy Sandhurst and its Predecessors, Country Life Books (1980) page 29.

5. The Adjutant General referred to a "dangerous spirit of Jacobinism" at the College, quoted in Heathcote op.cit. page 11.

6. . Heathcote op.cit. page14

7. Yardley, Michael, Sandhurst: A documentary, Harrap (1987) page 24.

8. This transcript and the information about Butler's family is contained in a ts note from a descendant of Reverend Richard Butler found in the Sandhurst Collection's correspondence files.

9. Paget's witness statement in Minutes of Evidence respecting the Conduct of the Lieutenant Governor of the Royal Military College at Sandhurst, 24<sup>th</sup> April 1828, page12 in WO99/25 Box 30

10. Letter from the Secretary to Commissioners to Hon General Sir Edward Paget, GCB, dated 3 April 1828 in WO 99/26 Box 31

11. Butler's defence is contained in an untitled manuscript of 64 pages held with the other trial material under WO 99/25/12 Box 30

12. I have not gone into the detail of many of the minor charges brought by Cassigne (but see "The Following Statement of Abuses in the Royal Military College......submitted to the Governor's consideration" by Cassaigne, undated in WO 99/25 Box 30), that Butler in his reply described as "embracing every paltry circumstance that slander and hatred could invent or distort" Butler op.cit. page 1, as most of them are merely further illustrations of the major charges. The following is drawn from the report of the trial in The Minutes of the Proceedings of the Supreme Board of the Royal Military College held at the Horse Guards 17<sup>th</sup> April 1828, Minutes of Evidence respecting the Conduct of the Lieutenant Governor of the Royal Military

College at Sandhurst, 19th, 22nd, 24th and The Minutes of the Proceedings of the Supreme Board of the Royal Military College held at the Horse Guards 26th April 1828 and 2nd and 5th May 1828 in WO99/25 Box 30.

13. Butler's defence op.cit. page 15.

14. Minutes of the proceedings of the Supreme Board of the Royal Military College, Horse Guards 29th March 1828 pages 11 and 12.

15. Butler op. cit. page 46.

16. Butler op. cit. page 40

17.Butler did not comment on the wording of his letters to the parents of GCs Dixon and Tobin, but argued that the fact that he had allowed a clerk to copy the letters and put them in the Lieutenant Governor's official letter book showed that he was not acting improperly! Butler op.cit. page 7.

18. Statement of Abuses in the Royal Military College op.cit. page 1

Butler claimed that he had recommended to parents even before Laybourne's marriage that they should not leave their sons at the College during vacations to prevent the "forming low intimacies in the neighbourhood" Butler op. cit. page 6.

20.Unpublished manuscript held in the Sandhurst Collection.

21.Butler op.cit. pages 20-24. He claimed that he maintained four servants (Footman, Groom, Gardener and Under Gardener) while only being given an allowance for one, and that he needed all these servants, together with the occasional help of College servants, because of his status and because people were always knocking on his door concerning College business, which meant that he had to keep one servant solely for the purpose of opening the door. He also argued that his allotment was helping to improve the Sandhurst Estate. He admitted that he had used one College servant as his personal servant during a trip to Bath, but that this had taken place during the Summer recess.

22. The note in the Staff register is unclear, but it seems to be implying that Cassaigne left for health reasons.

23. Paget op.cit. page 19.

24.Butler even boasted that he brought forward orphans for consideration by the examiners for a commission, if there conduct was good, even if they were "very deficient in ability", Butler op.cit. page 12.

25.The following account is based on the material contained in the manuscript

Minutes of the proceedings of the Supreme Board of the Royal Military College held at Sandhurst on 9th Of December 1828 and Minutes of Evidence taken before the Supreme Board of Commissioners of the Royal Military College at the College at Sandhurst Wednesday 10th December and Thursday 11th December 1828. WO99/27

26.Minutes of the Evidence taken before the Supreme Board of Commissioners of the Royal Military College at the College at Sandhurst Thursday 11th December 1828 page 203.

27.Minutes of the Evidence taken before the Supreme Board of Commissioners of the Royal Military College at the College at Sandhurst Wednesday 10th December 1828 page 34. The Reverend William Hancock also stated in evidence that he noticed the "jealous spirit" between the military and academics as soon as he came to the RMC in January 1813, Minutes of Evidence page 109.

28. Findings of the Supreme Board of Commissioners 17 December 1828 WO/99/27

29. This information was passed to the author by the Reverend Ian Blyth, Assistant Priest of St Lawrences, West Woodhay during a telephone conversation and exchange of emails in May 2007.

30. The full text of the memorial (seen by the author in July 2007) reads "To the memory of Lt General James Butler of the Royal Horse Artillery and late Lieutenant Governor of the Royal Military College at Sandhurst who died on the 18th August in the year of our Lord 1836 aged 74 years. This tablet was erected as a testimony of regard by his widow".

The Author

Dr Peter Thwaites was Curator of the Sandhurst Collection from 1998 until 2009